CHECKERBOARD SOCIAL STUDIES LIBRARY

DEFENDING THE NATION

Defending the Nation

THE MARINE CORPS

John Hamilton

ABDO Publishing Company

visit us at
www.abdopublishing.com

Published by ABDO Publishing Company, 4940 Viking Drive, Edina, Minnesota 55435.
Copyright © 2007 by Abdo Consulting Group, Inc. International copyrights reserved in all
countries. No part of this book may be reproduced in any form without written permission from
the publisher. The Checkerboard Library™ is a trademark and logo of ABDO Publishing
Company.

Printed in the United States.

Cover Photos: front, Corbis; back, U.S. Air Force
Interior Photos: Corbis pp. 1, 11, 12; Getty Images pp. 14, 15, 23; North Wind pp. 8, 9; U.S. Air
  Force p. 17; U.S. Department of Defense pp. 20-21; U.S. Marine Corps pp. 5, 18, 19, 21, 22,
  24, 25, 26-27, 29

Series Coordinator: Megan M. Gunderson
Editors: Heidi M. Dahmes, Megan M. Gunderson
Art Direction & Cover Design: Neil Klinepier

Library of Congress Cataloging-in-Publication Data

Hamilton, John, 1959-
  The Marine Corps / John Hamilton.
    p. cm. -- (Defending the nation)
  Includes index.
  ISBN-13: 978-1-59679-758-1
  ISBN-10: 1-59679-758-4
  1. United States. Marine Corps--Juvenile literature. I. Title II. Series: Hamilton, John, 1959- .
Defending the nation.

  VE23.H292 2006
  359.9'60973--dc22

                                                    2005029133

Contents

The U.S. Marine Corps

The U.S. military is among the most powerful in the world. It exists to protect America and its people. The military is trained to defeat America's enemies. But it can also help victims of natural disasters. When hurricanes or earthquakes strike, the U.S. military is often there to help.

The Marine Corps is one branch of the U.S. military. It is part of the U.S. Department of the Navy. The Marine Corps works closely with the U.S. Navy. But, they are separate services.

The Marine Corps is smaller than the army, the navy, or the air force. And, it is the only U.S. armed force specially designed for military service abroad. Marines are stationed worldwide, ready to protect U.S. interests wherever a crisis arises.

Marines form one of the world's most **elite** fighting forces. The Marine Corps is an all-purpose military unit that specializes in **mobilizing** quickly and attacking **aggressively**. For this reason, it is often **deployed** before other armed forces. A famous motto of the marines is "First to Fight." In addition to their combat role, marines guard the White House, as well as U.S. **embassies** around the world.

4

It is the Marine Corps's job to help preserve the peace and security of the United States. Today, more than 170,000 people serve in the U.S. Marine Corps. The men and women of today's U.S. Marine Corps are volunteers. They willingly give their time, and sometimes their lives, to defend their country.

The Marine Corps's official colors are scarlet and gold. Its emblem is an eagle perched on top of a globe with an anchor behind it. These colors and symbols are all represented on the Marine Corps flag.

Timeline

1775 - On November 10, the Continental Congress created the Continental marines.

1783 - The Continental marines were disbanded.

1798 - On July 11, the U.S. Marine Corps was formed.

1805 - Marines stormed Derna, Tripoli.

1847 - The marines captured the National Palace in Mexico City, Mexico, during the Mexican War.

1918 - The marines fought in the battle of Belleau Wood.

1950 - Marines successfully carried out an amphibious landing at Inchon, South Korea, during the Korean War.

2003 - Marine forces helped defeat the Iraqi military and capture Iraq's capital city, Baghdad.

2004 - Marines launched fierce assaults on the city of al-Fallujah, Iraq.

2005 - General Peter Pace became the first marine to act as chairman of the Joint Chiefs of Staff.

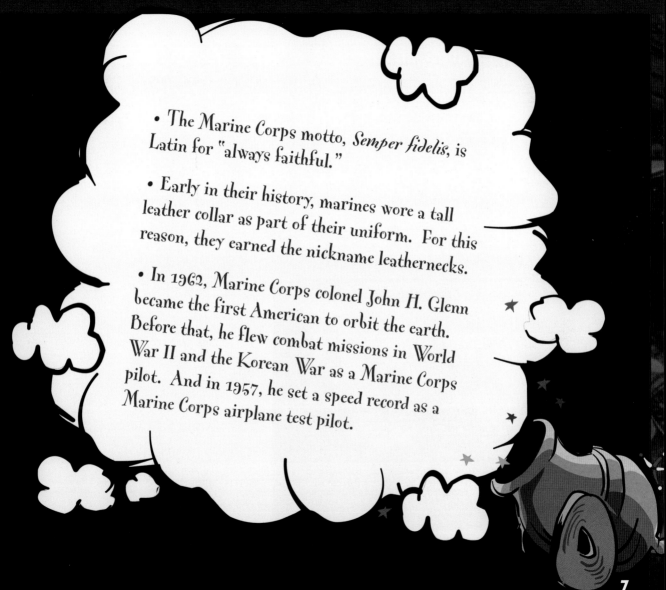

- The Marine Corps motto, *Semper fidelis*, is Latin for "always faithful."

- Early in their history, marines wore a tall leather collar as part of their uniform. For this reason, they earned the nickname leathernecks.

- In 1962, Marine Corps colonel John H. Glenn became the first American to orbit the earth. Before that, he flew combat missions in World War II and the Korean War as a Marine Corps pilot. And in 1957, he set a speed record as a Marine Corps airplane test pilot.

During the **Revolutionary War**, the **Continental Congress** governed the American colonies. On November 10, 1775, Congress created the Continental marines. The marines were stationed aboard Continental navy ships.

After the war, the Continental marines were no longer needed. So, the force was **disbanded** in 1783. But, the new nation needed protection, even in peacetime. So on July 11, 1798, the U.S. Congress authorized the formation of the U.S. Marine Corps.

The Continental Congress met in Philadelphia, Pennsylvania.

However, marines still celebrate November 10, 1775, as their official birthday.

The Marine Corps has fought in every U.S. naval action. Two conflicts in the 1800s remain especially important in marine

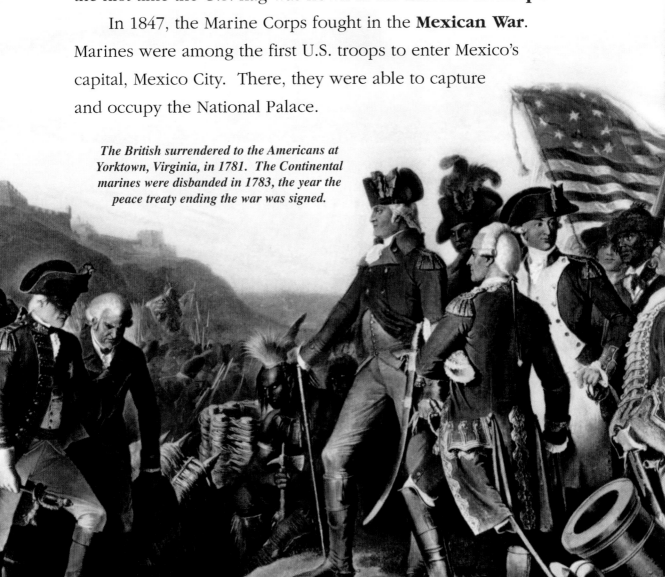

history. In 1805, a group of marines stormed Derna, Tripoli. It was the first time the U.S. flag was flown in the **Eastern Hemisphere**.

In 1847, the Marine Corps fought in the **Mexican War**. Marines were among the first U.S. troops to enter Mexico's capital, Mexico City. There, they were able to capture and occupy the National Palace.

The British surrendered to the Americans at Yorktown, Virginia, in 1781. The Continental marines were disbanded in 1783, the year the peace treaty ending the war was signed.

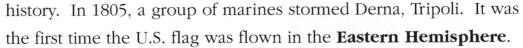

The Marine Corps has been sent to many countries in times of crisis. Marines served as infantry, or ground troops, in countries such as Nicaragua, China, and Haiti in the early 1900s.

In June 1918, the Marine Corps participated in the battle of Belleau Wood. This **World War I** battle took place north of Paris, France, as the German military tried to advance on the capital. The corps fought hard and was victorious. Marines earned a reputation for being tough and persistent. The battle of Belleau Wood is remembered as the bloodiest fight in corps history up to that point.

Following World War I, the Marine Corps's military role began to change. The Marine Corps began to focus much more on being an amphibious assault force. This meant marines were specially trained to invade enemy shores from navy ships.

During **World War II**, the U.S. Marine Corps launched many amphibious attacks against the Japanese. Fierce battles took place on Pacific islands, including Guadalcanal, Tarawa, Iwo Jima, and Okinawa. During that time, a marine **aviation** team was also used to support ground, sea, and amphibious operations. Marine Corps aviators downed about 2,300 Japanese aircraft.

Honoring Heroism

In February and March 1945, U.S. and Japanese armed forces fought each other in the battle of Iwo Jima. More than 20,000 Japanese soldiers defended the island with an elaborate system of caves and tunnels. The battle raged for more than a month before the Marine Corps took control of the island.

More than 70,000 marines fought in this important World War II battle. About 5,900 marines were killed, and more than 17,000 were wounded.

During the battle of Iwo Jima, a group of marines raised the U.S. flag on top of Mount Suribachi. A photograph was taken of the event. It came to symbolize the fighting spirit of the U.S. Marine Corps.

Sculptor Felix W. de Weldon designed a statue based on the photograph. And, Horace W. Peaslee designed a memorial. In 1954, the Marine Corps War Memorial was dedicated in Washington, D.C.

REBELLION·1900★NICARAGUA·1912★VERA·CRUZ·1914★HAITI·1915-1934★SANTO·DOMINGO·1916-1924★WORLD·WAR·I·1917-1918·BELLEAU·WOOD·SOISSONS·ST

IN·HONOR·AND·MEMORY

After **World War II**, the United States continued to rely on the marines. The corps performed an especially important role in the **Korean War**. In 1950, marines successfully carried out an amphibious landing behind enemy lines at Inchon, South Korea. This led in part to South Korea's eventual freedom from North Korea.

In the **Vietnam War**, marines were part of the first U.S. combat units **deployed**. More marines served and more died in this war than in World War II. After the United States withdrew from Vietnam, the corps participated in smaller conflicts around the world. And, marines continued to provide assistance to many nations during natural disasters.

During the 2003 U.S. invasion of Iraq, light, fast-moving forces like the marines were needed to defeat the Iraqi military. Marines helped capture Baghdad, the capital of Iraq. And, they fought many battles following the invasion. Marines launched especially fierce assaults on the city of al-Fallujah in 2004.

The November 2004 assault on al-Fallujah was called Operation al-Fajr.

In 2005, the Marine Corps celebrated its 230th birthday. As a tribute, four Marine Corps leaders were featured on U.S. postage stamps. Sergeant Major Daly was one of the honored leaders.

Many marine commanders have bravely led their troops into battle. Some have received the Medal of Honor. This is the highest military award given by the United States. It is awarded for actions "above and beyond the call of duty." Sergeant Major Daniel "Dan" Daly received the Medal of Honor twice. Only two marines have ever received two such medals.

Daly received his first Medal of Honor for service in China in 1900. He received the second one after serving in Haiti in 1915. But, Daly is best remembered for his leadership during the battle of Belleau Wood. He was awarded the Navy Cross for his heroism during this battle.

General Peter Pace is a four-star general. Pace served in combat during the **Vietnam War**. And, he has held Marine Corps jobs all over the world.

In 2005, Pace became the first marine to serve as chairman of the Joint Chiefs of Staff. This military advisory group includes a leader from each branch of the U.S. armed forces. The chairman advises the president, the secretary of defense, and the National Security Council about the military.

General Pace graduated from the U.S. Naval Academy in 1967. Since then, he has received numerous medals for his service in the Marine Corps.

Organization

Each branch of the U.S. military is organized by a hierarchy. This means there are many levels of responsibility. So, some people have more authority than others.

The head of the U.S. military is the president of the United States. He or she is called the commander in chief. The highest-ranking member of the Marine Corps is the commandant of the Marine Corps. He or she is also a member of the Joint Chiefs of Staff.

Under the commandant of the Marine Corps are commissioned officers, warrant officers, noncommissioned officers, and **enlisted** marines. Officers have more responsibility than enlisted marines. They make important decisions and are specially trained in leadership skills. Officers also give orders to enlisted marines and to lower-ranking officers.

Noncommissioned officers fulfill leadership roles. They are enlisted marines who have achieved the rank of corporal or above. Enlisted marines hold ranks below officers. They enter the Marine Corps as privates.

Ranks

Officer Ranks

Second Lieutenant (O-1)

First Lieutenant (O-2)

Captain (O-3)

Major (O-4)

Lieutenant Colonel (O-5)

Colonel (O-6)

Brigadier General (O-7)

Major General (O-8)

Lieutenant General (O-9)

General (O-10)

Warrant Officer Ranks

Warrant Officer 1 (W-1)

Chief Warrant Officer 2 (W-2)

Chief Warrant Officer 3 (W-3)

Chief Warrant Officer 4 (W-4)

Chief Warrant Officer 5 (W-5)

Enlisted Ranks

Private (E-1)

Private First Class (E-2)

Lance Corporal (E-3)

Corporal (E-4)

Sergeant (E-5)

Staff Sergeant (E-6)

Gunnery Sergeant (E-7)

Master Sergeant (E-8)

First Sergeant (E-8)

Sergeant Major (E-9)

Master Gunnery Sergeant (E-9)

Sergeant Major of the Marine Corps (E-9)

The letter and number next to each rank indicates a person's pay grade.

Training

To **enlist** in the Marine Corps, a person must be between 17 and 28 years old. Candidates also need to be high school graduates.

Enlisted marines, or recruits, begin training at a Marine Corps Recruit Depot. These training centers are located in both San Diego, California, and Parris Island, South Carolina. Training, or boot camp, lasts for 13 weeks. During this time, recruits become physically fit and learn how to take orders.

Because of the many duties marines are called on to fulfill, the corps stresses combat training. Marines also become skilled in shooting rifles. And, they are highly trained in hand-to-hand combat, such as martial arts.

Marines take either the oath of enlistment or the oath of office to join the corps.

After graduating from boot camp, some **enlisted** marines enter the School of Infantry (SOI) West at Camp Pendleton, California. Others enter the SOI East at Camp Geiger, North Carolina. At SOI, infantry marines enter an Infantry Training Battalion to learn more about their Military Occupational Specialty (MOS). An MOS is a marine's job. Non-infantry marines enter a Marine Combat Training Battalion at SOI instead. After SOI, these marines enter an MOS school for training that relates to the specific job they are assigned.

Weapons training includes learning to keep guns well maintained and clean for inspections.

There is more than one way to become a commissioned officer in the U.S. Marine Corps. If a person already has a college degree, he or she may begin training at the Officer Candidates School (OCS) at Marine Corps Base Quantico in Virginia. Upon graduation, an officer's starting rank is second lieutenant.

Another way to become an officer is through a service academy such as the U.S. Naval Academy. Founded in 1845, this school educates future officers of both the navy and the Marine Corps. The **Enlisted** Commissioning Program also provides options for becoming a commissioned officer. The program allows enlisted marines with a college degree to apply for OCS.

Upon receiving their commission, all marine officers must attend The Basic

School (TBS). This six-month program is also located at Quantico. TBS teaches officers how to effectively lead and command marines. Candidates also study map reading, weapons, and Marine Corps history.

As they near graduation from TBS, officers choose an MOS. Options include communications, artillery, and combat engineering. Some marines also move on to highly specialized training. This includes studying law and learning to fly jets.

OCS tasks include obstacle courses and combat training.

Marine Corps Reserve

There are several other ways to train for and participate in the U.S. Marine Corps. One option is the Naval Reserve Officers' Training Corps (ROTC). The navy and the Marine Corps have a close relationship. So, the

Naval ROTC midshipmen receive training outside the classroom in subjects such as navigation.

Naval ROTC trains future officers for both branches.

More than 160 U.S. colleges have Naval ROTC programs. While attending college, Naval ROTC students, or midshipmen, take additional courses in naval science. And during the summer, midshipmen receive extra training. This includes six weeks at OCS. Upon graduation, midshipmen are commissioned as second lieutenants in the Marine Corps Reserve.

The Marine Corps Reserve is yet another part of the U.S. Marine Corps. Reserve marines choose an MOS and are then trained to be marines. But, they continue to hold regular jobs or attend school outside of the military.

Each reservist trains one weekend a month near his or her home. Reserve marines also serve two weeks every summer. This annual training could take place on a ship. Reservists are ready to be called to action whenever and wherever the Marine Corps needs assistance.

Since the U.S.-led invasion in 2003, thousands of reserve marines have been called to action to assist in Iraq.

Weapons

When marines are ready to go on a mission, marine aircraft can quickly drop them into combat zones. Marines have used the CH-46 Sea Knight longer than any other helicopter. Sea Knights can transport marines from one base to another, or from ship to shore. Depending on the **terrain**, marines may even use ropes to either **rappel** or fast rope from the helicopter. These are different methods for using ropes to exit a helicopter without it landing.

Marines are trained to fast rope from CH-46 Sea Knights on land and at sea.

Another transport helicopter is the CH-53E Super Stallion. This important vehicle can lift more weight than any other helicopter. It carries marines anywhere they need to go. And, it can even be refuelled while in flight! This extends the distance a Super Stallion can travel.

Other aircraft support marines once they are on the

F/A-18 Hornets

ground. Marine aircraft include the F/A-18 Hornet. This assault airplane flies nearly twice the speed of sound. Marines also use the AV-8B Harrier jet, which can take off and land like a helicopter. And, the Marine Corps uses the AH-1 Cobra. This attack helicopter also supports ground troops.

Marines are also prepared for amphibious landings. At these times, an Amphibious Assault Vehicle (AAV) is often put to use. The AAV transports up to 21 marines from ship to shore. Marines can then drive the vehicle as much as 400 miles (640 km) inland.

The Landing Craft Air Cushion (LCAC) is also used for transporting weapons and personnel from ship to shore. The LCAC was made to carry heavy loads at high speeds. It can even transport a 67-ton (61-t) M1A1 tank!

On the ground, marines use a variety of individual weapons. Every

marine is expected to be an expert rifleman. The reliable, lightweight M16 is the standard rifle used by U.S. Marines. The semi-automatic M9 Beretta pistol is another standard weapon for many marines. Even when loaded, it weighs only 2.55 pounds (1.16 kg). Other advanced technology helps marines once they reach land. Marines use night vision goggles to see in the dark. This allows them to accomplish missions even at night. Ground troops also use MK19 40mm grenade launchers. These weapons can fire 350 grenades in a single minute!

Marines have used night vision goggles when patrolling Iraqi streets after dark.

The Future of the Marine Corps

Several times in its history, the U.S. government has threatened to **disband** the Marine Corps. Yet, the marines have always survived these pressures to shut down.

Most people recognize the value of a quick-strike force that can fight throughout the world. To fight in many of today's battlefields, smaller, faster forces are needed. This is especially true in the ongoing war on **terrorism** in Afghanistan and Iraq.

To be successful, marines must learn to respond quickly and forcefully to future threats. Marines are also skilled at keeping the peace once a battle is won. The Marine Corps has some of the best-trained fighters and most advanced technology at its fingertips. Because of this, the U.S. Marine Corps will be ready for whatever the future holds.

U.S. marines have a history of helping humanitarian efforts. They helped provide food for victims of the 2004 Asian tsunami.

Glossary

aggressive - displaying hostility.

aviation - the operation and navigation of aircraft. A person that operates an aircraft is called an aviator.

Continental Congress - the body of representatives that spoke for and acted on behalf of the 13 colonies.

deploy - to send out and organize in battle formation.

disband - to break up something that is organized.

Eastern Hemisphere - one half of the earth east of the Atlantic Ocean, including Europe, Africa, Asia, and Australia.

elite (ih-LEET) - of or relating to the best part of a class.

embassy - the home and office of a diplomat who lives in a foreign country.

enlist - to join the armed forces voluntarily. An enlistee is a person who enlists for military service.

Korean War - from 1950 to 1953. A war between North and South Korea. The U.S. government sent troops to help South Korea.

Mexican War - from 1846 to 1848. A war between the United States and Mexico.

mobilize - to assemble and make ready for action, especially related to war.

rappel (ruh-PEHL) - to lower oneself down a rope, often from a cliff or a helicopter.

Revolutionary War - from 1775 to 1783. A war for independence between Great Britain and its North American colonies. The colonists won and created the United States of America.

Glossary

terrain - the physical features of an area of land. Mountains, rivers, and canyons can all be part of a terrain.

terrorism - the use of terror, violence, or threats to frighten people into action. A person who commits an act of terrorism is called a terrorist.

Vietnam War - from 1957 to 1975. A long, failed attempt by the United States to stop North Vietnam from taking over South Vietnam.

World War I - from 1914 to 1918, fought in Europe. Great Britain, France, Russia, the United States, and their allies were on one side. Germany, Austria-Hungary, and their allies were on the other side.

World War II - from 1939 to 1945, fought in Europe, Asia, and Africa. Great Britain, France, the United States, the Soviet Union, and their allies were on one side. Germany, Italy, Japan, and their allies were on the other side.

Web Sites

To learn more about the U.S. Marine Corps, visit ABDO Publishing Company on the World Wide Web at **www.abdopublishing.com**. Web sites about the U.S. Marine Corps are featured on our Book Links page. These links are routinely monitored and updated to provide the most current information available.

Index